Page 35
Pg. 54

GIANTS OF THE OLD TESTAMENT

LESSONS ON LIVING FROM

ESTHER

Living Courageously in Difficult Days

A devotional by

WOODROW KROLL

BACK TO THE BIBLE®
Lincoln, Nebraska

15,200 printed to date—1997
(117-0226—15.2M—47)
ISBN 0-8474-0679-2

Printed in the United States of America.

CONTENTS

DAY 1

Esther 1:1, 3-4

Now it came to pass in the days of Ahasuerus (this was the Ahasuerus who reigned over one hundred and twenty-seven provinces, from India to Ethiopia), . . . that in the third year of his reign he made a feast for all his officials and servants—the powers of Persia and Media, the nobles, and the princes of the provinces being before him—when he showed the riches of his glorious kingdom and the splendor of his excellent majesty for many days, one hundred and eighty days in all.

Happiness Is . . .

A number of years ago a popular fad was to complete the phrase "Happiness is . . . ." Some suggested that happiness is a cuddly warm puppy; others said happiness is having good health, a comfortable home, money in the bank, a close family or loyal friends.

Had someone asked the Persian king Ahasuerus about happiness, he probably would have answered, "Victory in battle." Ahasuerus was gearing up to wage war against Greece. It wasn't that he needed more land; at its height the Persian Empire controlled nearly two million square miles. Nor did he need more wealth. It took 180 days for Ahasuerus to display all his possessions. None of this, however, made him happy.

4

Esther 1:4

Ahasuerus later failed in his attempt to conquer the Greeks. He was defeated at the battle of Salamis and retreated home to lick his wounds. It wouldn't have mattered anyway. True happiness can no more be found in military victory than in material possessions. Instead, as the children's song expresses it, "Happiness is to know the Savior, living a life within His favor, having a change in my behavior. Happiness is the Lord."

What are you looking to for happiness? Family, friends and sufficient material possessions are important. But knowing that your sins are forgiven and you're on your way to heaven is real happiness. If you haven't received Jesus Christ as your Savior, do so today. If you already have a personal relationship with the Lord, take a few moments to meditate on all your blessings.

Success is getting what you want; happiness is wanting what you get.

Reflections/Prayer Requests

_____

_____

_____

_____

DAY 2

Esther 1:10-12

*On the seventh day, when the heart of
the king was merry with wine, he commanded
Mehuman, Biztha, Harbona, Bigtha, Abagtha,
Zethar, and Carcas, <u>seven</u> eunuchs who served
in the presence of King Ahasuerus, to bring
Queen Vashti before the king, wearing her royal
crown, in order to show her beauty to the people and the officials, for she was beautiful to
behold. But Queen Vashti refused to come at
the king's command brought by his eunuchs;
therefore the king was furious,
and his anger burned within him.*

Standing Firm

Thomas Jefferson wrote, "In matters of
style, swim with the current; in matters of
principle, stand like a rock." In other words,
some things are not worth arguing about,
while others are of such value they cannot
be compromised.

Although a pagan queen, Vashti had
principles she refused to compromise.
When Ahasuerus called for her to present
herself before his comrades and him,
Vashti knew it was inappropriate in her culture for a woman to display herself to the
leers of other men. To expose herself to
such treatment implied an immodesty,
even an unchastity, that was not true of

her. She would not concede her principles and thus refused the king's command.

Standing for one's principles, however, can have costly consequences. Vashti was removed from her position as queen. Others have made similar sacrifices. Bubba Smith, regarded as one of professional football's greatest defensive ends, chose to end a lucrative contract to do beer commercials because he concluded that they encouraged the wrong kind of behavior.

Whether at work, in social relationships, or in the political arena, Christians face tremendous pressure to participate in activities and attitudes contrary to God's will. It's important, however, that we take an uncompromising position when it comes to our principles.

Ask God to give you the ability to discern between what is merely incidental and what is of eternal value. Then ask Him to give you the strength and courage to stand for your principles.

Tolerance is often championed by people who have nothing to stand for.

Reflections/Prayer Requests

DAY 3

Esther 1:17-18

*"For the queen's behavior
will become known to all women,
so that they will despise their husbands in
their eyes, when they report, 'King Ahasuerus
commanded Queen Vashti to be brought in
before him, but she did not come.'
This very day the noble ladies of Persia
and Media will say to all the king's officials
that they have heard of the behavior
of the queen. Thus there will be
excessive contempt and wrath."*

Keep Your Cool

Overreacting can have unexpected results. One mother related that she came home from a shopping trip to find her five children in a huddle. Curious as to what could be so intriguing, she slipped up behind them and peeked over their shoulders. To her horror she saw the kids had captured five baby skunks. "Quick, children, run!" she shouted. Thinking some disaster was about to happen, they scattered to all parts of the house—each with a baby skunk in his arms. The mother's overreaction insured that every room got its share of the spray.

When King Ahasuerus' advisors overreacted, they created an equally odious situa-

8

tion. What could have been merely a personal family matter was blown into an issue of national security. Consequently, their suggestion to remove Vashti as queen (v. 19) far exceeded the crime.

Often the intensity of the moment causes situations to loom far larger than they really are. When we overreact to such circumstances, sometimes justice gets trampled in the stampede. Then we regret our responses when we later view them more objectively.

Are there things in your life that seem unbearable? Does someone always rub you the wrong way? Before you overreact, ask God to show you His purpose in your frustrations. View them with eternity's telescope. Get God's viewpoint before you react.

A moment of prayerful reflection can prevent a lifetime of bitter regret.

Reflections/Prayer Requests

_____

_____

_____

_____

_____

DAY 4

Esther 1:20-22

"When the king's decree which he will make is proclaimed throughout all his empire (for it is great), all wives will honor their husbands, both great and small." And the reply pleased the king and the princes, and the king did according to the word of Memucan. Then he sent letters to all the king's provinces, to each province in its own script, and to every people in their own language, that each man should be master in his own house, and speak in the language of his own people.

Standing on the Inside

A little boy misbehaved until finally his mother told him to go sit in the corner. Reluctantly he went to the corner, but he refused to sit. "David," his mother said firmly, "I told you to sit in the corner, not stand." David remained standing. "David, I said sit." The boy stood stubbornly. Finally, the mother came over, placed her hands firmly on his shoulder and sat him in his chair. As she turned to leave, however, she heard him say softly to himself, "I may be sitting on the outside, but I'm standing on the inside."

Force can create outward compliance, but it can't change inward attitudes. King Ahasuerus was the most powerful man in the Persian Empire. His edict was law. No one dared disobey him outwardly. When the proclamation came demanding that wives respect their husbands, you can be sure there was outward obedience, but nothing changed on the inside.

Scripture says, "Nevertheless let each one of you in particular so love his own wife as himself, and let the wife see that she respects her husband" (Eph. 5:33). Notice that respect follows love. Unless a husband is satisfied with just outward conformity, he has to earn that respect by loving his wife, treating her fairly and kindly and exercising godly leadership in his family.

If you are a wife, treat your husband with the respect desired by God. If you are a husband, prove you are worthy of your wife's respect by the way you treat her. You can never enjoy respect by demanding it, but you can earn it.

When respect is earned, it will first be evident on the inside.

Reflections/Prayer Requests

_____

_____

_____

DAY 5

Esther 2:1

After these things, when the wrath of King Ahasuerus subsided, he remembered Vashti, what she had done, and what had been decreed against her.

Vain Regret

A man never opened the car door for his wife nor did any of the other little niceties that wives appreciate. He felt such a show of chivalry was silly. "Besides," he said, "she doesn't have two broken arms." This went on for many years until finally his wife died. At the funeral, the family waited at the hearse for the pallbearers. When they came, the mortician called the husband by name and asked, "Open the door for her, will you?" The man reached for the door handle and suddenly froze. Regret came crashing in on him. He realized he had never opened the car door for her in her life; now in her death it would be the first, last and only time.

How painful such regrets can be. King Ahasuerus experienced them when he came to his senses and realized how foolish he had been in banishing Queen Vashti. His regrets were in vain, however, because the law of the Medes and the Persians could not be changed. For the rest of his life he would live with the remorse of having wronged his queen.

Rare is the individual who makes it through life without having said or done something he regrets. If it's within our power, we should right such wrongs. An apology, a change in behavior, even an offer of restitution may take the sting out of our regrets. But sometimes it won't happen; sometimes it's just too late.

As Christians, we must live so as to minimize regrets. And when we experience them, we should be quick to ask for God's forgiveness and for forgiveness from those we wrong. Let's live by the Galatians 6:10 principle: "Therefore, as we have opportunity, let us do good to all, especially to those who are of the household of faith."

Live thoughtfully today and you won't have to live regretfully tomorrow.

Reflections/Prayer Requests

_____

_____

_____

_____

_____

DAY 6

Esther 2:7

And Mordecai had brought up Hadassah,
that is, Esther, his uncle's daughter,
for she had neither father nor mother.
The young woman was lovely and beautiful.
When her father and mother died,
Mordecai took her as his own daughter.

Family Values

One of the most monumental works in all the world is the Great Wall of China. It stretches more than 1,500 miles over mountains and deserts and is the only man-made structure visible from space. The Chinese built it to keep out barbarians, and for the most part they succeeded. Only three times was it ever breeched, and in all three instances the enemy gained access by bribing a gatekeeper. Even the strongest security system is worthless if those responsible do not have appropriate values.

It is evident that Mordecai had strong values. Scripture reveals that while Esther was still young, her parents died and Modecai took her into his home and raised her as though she were his own daughter. While in his home, Esther learned the values of loyalty, obedience and courage, all of which she would need to intercede for her people.

When values deteriorate, so does everything else. Former American President Ronald Reagan observed, "If we fail to instruct our children in justice, religion, and liberty, we will be condemning them to a world without virtue, a life in the twilight of a civilization where the great truths have been forgotten."

Take seriously your responsibility to teach those in your house the values that make life worthwhile. Share the Word of God with your children and grandchildren as the source of those values. Teach them to "do according to all that is written in it" so that it may go well with their lives (Josh. 1:8).

A life empty of values is a life without value.

Reflections/Prayer Requests

_____

_____

_____

_____

_____

_____

DAY 7

Esther 2:8-9

*So it was, when the king's command and decree were heard, and when many young women were gathered at Shushan the citadel, under the custody of Hegai, that Esther also was taken to the king's palace, into the care of Hegai the custodian of the women.
Now the young woman pleased him, and she obtained his favor; so he readily gave beauty preparations to her, besides her allowance.
Then seven choice maidservants were provided for her from the king's palace, and he moved her and her maidservants to the best place in the house of the women.*

Make Lemonade

Those who find the greatest joy in life are people who refuse to be discouraged by their circumstances. Author Zig Ziglar says, "If life hands you a lemon, take the lemon and make lemonade."

Esther was handed a lemon. King Ahasuerus decreed that all the beautiful young virgins in his kingdom should be brought to Shushan for his inspection. He was looking for a new queen, and a beauty pageant was his method of choice. Esther was part of these degrading procedures. But in spite of what must have been an ordeal for a young Jewish woman, she kept her sweet spirit. Her attitude so impressed Hegai, the custodian of the women, that she became a favorite.

Others have learned this secret as well. Charles Goodyear's lemon was a prison sentence resulting from a contempt of court citation. Instead of complaining, he became an assistant in the kitchen. He then used this sour situation to work on an idea for vulcanizing rubber. His lemon became our lemonade. Because of Charles Goodyear, we have better tires, which means better travel and a better way of life.

God doesn't exempt us from experiencing sour fruit. We live in a fallen world and that means we may find ourselves in situations as tart as lemons. But God can help us keep our spirits sweet. Ask Him to help you. A sweet testimony can squeeze the juice out of a sour world.

⬡

Nothing is so sour that it can't be sweetened by a good attitude.

Reflections/Prayer Requests

_____

_____

_____

_____

_____

DAY 8

Esther 2:12

Each young woman's turn came
to go in to King Ahasuerus after she had
completed twelve months' preparation,
according to the regulations for the women,
for thus were the days of their preparation
apportioned: six months with oil of myrrh,
and six months with perfumes and
preparations for beautifying women.

Preparing for the King

To many Nebraskans, football is king. Every game at the University of Nebraska takes a lot of preparation. Two days before the game 25 people meet to plan their strategies for ensuring that everything runs smoothly. Game day begins at 3:30 A.M. for a 1:00 P.M. kickoff. In the following hours concession deliveries provide for 10,000 slices of pizza, 20,000 hot dogs, 60,000 drinks and a half ton of popcorn. Security details make multiple sweeps of the stadium; electricians and plumbers activate the necessary systems; identification checkers take up their posts; and various police units prepare to respond to any emergency. Before the day is over, some workers will have put in more than 14 hours of preparation.

Yet all these preparations are nothing

18

compared with those endured by the women chosen to meet the king of Persia. For six months they bathed in oil of myrrh. For another six months they soaked in perfumes just to be ready when their time came to meet Ahasuerus.

Christians also have an appointment with their King. The apostle Paul speaks of that moment when "we who are alive and remain shall be caught up together with them in the clouds to meet the Lord in the air. And thus we shall always be with the Lord" (1 Thess. 4:17). What a glorious moment that will be!

But now is the time to prepare. Today is all we have to earn the right to be called "good and faithful servants." Yesterday is gone; tomorrow may never come. Seize your opportunities today.

You have eternity to enjoy the honeymoon, but only a short time to prepare for the wedding.

Reflections/Prayer Requests

_____

_____

_____

_____

_____

DAY 9

Esther 2:15

*Now when the turn came for Esther
the daughter of Abihail the uncle of Mordecai,
who had taken her as his daughter, to go in to
the king, she requested nothing but what
Hegai the king's eunuch, the custodian of the
women, advised. And Esther obtained favor
in the sight of all who saw her.*

Inner Beauty

American culture puts a lot of emphasis on outer beauty. Each year, Americans collectively buy per minute 1,484 tubes of lipstick (at a cost of $4,566); 913 bottles of nail polish ($2,055); 1,324 mascaras, eyeshadows, and eyeliners ($6,849); and 2,055 jars of skin care products ($12,785). Marketing beauty products to both men and women represents an almost $17 billion-per-year business in the U.S.

This is far different from the example of Esther. Despite the fact that her future seemed to depend on making a favorable impression on the king, she did no more than what was necessary to appear appropriate. Without the distraction of the glitz and glamour of outer beauty aids, her inner beauty could be clearly seen. And it was this inner beauty that enabled Esther to obtain "favor in the sight of all who saw her," including the king, who eventually made her queen.

There is nothing wrong with wanting to appear attractive, but it should never be our primary concern. Developing inner beauty is far more important. The writer of Proverbs says, "Who can find a virtuous wife? For her worth is far above rubies" (31:10). And the apostle Peter says, "Do not let your adornment be merely outward; arranging the hair, wearing gold, or putting on fine apparel; rather let it be the hidden person of the heart, with the incorruptible beauty of a gentle and quiet spirit, which is very precious in the sight of God" (1 Peter 3:3-4).

If you want real beauty, spend as much time before the mirror of God's Word as you do before the mirror in your bathroom. Let God develop an inner beauty in you that will both outshine and outlast the glamour of the world.

Beauty without virtue is like a flower without fragrance.

Reflections/Prayer Requests

DAY 10

Esther 2:20

*Now Esther had not yet revealed her family and
her people, just as Mordecai had charged her,
for Esther obeyed the command of Mordecai
as when she was brought up by him.*

The Habit of Obedience

A Roman centurion was instructed to
deliver a message. In order to reach his
destination he had to go through some very
dangerous territories. One of his soldiers
approached him and said, "Sir, if you try to
deliver this message, you'll be killed." The
centurion looked at the young man and
replied, "Soldier, it's not necessary for me
to live—it's only necessary for me to obey."

The Bible stresses the virtue of obeying
those who are in authority (Rom. 13:1). But
respect for authority begins in the home.
Mordecai raised Esther to be obedient—a
trait that she carried into adulthood. It was
her habit of obedience that made the difference when she needed to put her life on the
line for her people (Esther 4:15-16).

This kind of obedience needs to carry
over to our spiritual lives as well. If we do
not respectfully obey those whom we can
see, how can we expect to obey God, whom
we cannot see? How we respond to our par-

ents, teachers, employer, pastor, and elected officials is an excellent indicator of our attitude toward God.

Cultivate the habit of respectful obedience. When asked to do something that is not unethical or immoral and is consistent with godliness, respond cheerfully as "to the Lord" (Eph. 6:5-7). Your obedience to those in authority will set an example for others to follow, especially your children. Your obedience in daily matters also lays a foundation for those times when God calls you to obey in difficult circumstances. Make obedience a habit and you'll be prepared to face anything, large or small.

~~~

The key to godliness is not more knowledge but more obedience.

Reflections/Prayer Requests

_____

_____

_____

_____

_____

_____

_____

_____

DAY 11

Esther 2:21-23

In those days, while Mordecai sat within the king's gate, two of the king's eunuchs, Bigthan and Teresh, doorkeepers, became furious and sought to lay hands on King Ahasuerus. So the matter became known to Mordecai, who told Queen Esther, and Esther informed the king in Mordecai's name. And when an inquiry was made into the matter, it was confirmed, and both were hanged on a gallows; and it was written in the book of the chronicles in the presence of the king.

Because It's Right

John Stuart Mill (1806-1873) created a code of morality based on self-interest. He believed that only individuals and their particular interests were important, and those interests could be determined by whatever maximized their pleasure and minimized their pain.

This stands in stark contrast to the philosophy by which Mordecai lived. When Mordecai learned that a plot against the king's life was being planned, he immediately informed the king through Queen Esther. He risked everything, including the retaliation of the conspirator's families after the men were executed. And for what? His name was written in a book. No reward, no thanks. Although God eventually brought Mordecai's valor to the king's attention, for the moment the loyal Jew's only satisfaction was knowing he did what was right. But for Mordecai, knowing he had done the right thing was sufficient.

Our society in general lives by the standards expressed by John Stuart Mill. Someone summarized it in the expression "Get all you can. Can all you get." But God calls Christians to live selflessly. Today we may have to settle for the satisfaction of knowing what we have done is right; in the future, the God who keeps impeccable records will take care of the rewards.

Are you facing a thankless task? Are your efforts going unsung and unpraised? Don't be concerned. Do what you know is right and remember that, someday, your Heavenly Father will see to your rewards.

A man all wrapped up in himself makes a pretty small package.

Reflections/Prayer Requests

_____

_____

_____

_____

DAY 12

Esther 3:2-4

And all the king's servants who were within the king's gate bowed and paid homage to Haman, for so the king had commanded concerning him. But Mordecai would not bow or pay homage. Then the king's servants who were within the king's gate said to Mordecai, "Why do you transgress the king's command?" Now it happened, when they spoke to him daily and he would not listen to them, that they told it to Haman, to see whether Mordecai's words would stand; for Mordecai had told them that he was a Jew.

Not Ashamed

Frederick the Great invited some notable people, including his top-ranking generals, to a royal banquet. One of them, Hans von Zieten, declined the invitation because he wanted to partake of Communion at his church. Sometime later, at another banquet, Frederick and his guests mocked the Lord and the general for his religious scruples. Despite the peril to his life, the officer stood to his feet and said respectfully to the monarch, "My lord, there is a greater King than you, a King to whom I have sworn allegiance even unto death. I am a Christian, and I cannot sit quietly as the Lord's name is dishonored and His character belittled."

Instead of flying into a rage as the guests feared, the king grasped the hand of this courageous general and asked his forgiveness. He promised that he would never again allow a travesty to be made of sacred things.

Mordecai demonstrated the same courage. While he did not flaunt his Jewish heritage, neither was he ashamed of it. When push came to shove, he chose to be true to his faith rather than sacrifice it for the convenience of the moment. Even though it meant earning the enmity of the powerful Haman, Mordecai felt it was more important to stand for his beliefs than to be well-liked by his contemporaries.

Once it was Mordecai. Then it was Hans von Zieten. Now it's your turn. Are you willing to stand and be counted for your faith. Do your coworkers know you are a Christian by what you say and how you live? This is a time for action, not a time to be ashamed.

God has no place for undercover agents.

Reflections/Prayer Requests

DAY 13

Esther 3:5

*When Haman saw that Mordecai
did not bow or pay him homage,
Haman was filled with wrath.*

Focus on the Positive

A group of people were shown a large sheet of white cardboard with a small, black dot in the center. The leader of the group asked them, "What do you see?" Everyone responded that they saw a black dot. "Yes," replied the leader, "but what about all the white cardboard around it?"

It's easy to focus on the "black dot" and forget the rest. Haman did. We aren't told why, but he was elevated above all the other princes in the land (Esther 3:1). Since it took place shortly after the plot on the king's life was discovered, he may have taken credit for uncovering the scheme. Authority, wealth and recognition rolled into his coffers. He enjoyed having others bow and scrape before him, and it bothered him extremely when Mordecai refused to join the group. In fact, after sharing with his family and friends about all his wealth and honors, he concluded, "Yet all this avails me nothing, so long as I see Mordecai the Jew sitting at the king's gate" (Esther 5:13).

One negative outweighed all the positive.

How foolish we are when we allow a single flaw to destroy the many blessings that God has brought into our lives. We discredit our family when all we can see are their faults. We show disrespect for our pastor when we focus on his weakness and forget his many strengths. Most of all we do a disservice to God when all that is negative engulfs us and all that is positive escapes us.

Are you letting the negatives in your life outweigh the positives? Try focusing on all the good that comes from your circumstances and thank God for that. You may be gratified to discover that the "white space" in your life is far greater than the "black dot."

Concentrate on counting your blessings and you'll have little time to count anything else.

Reflections/Prayer Requests

_____

_____

_____

_____

_____

DAY 14

Esther 3:8-9

Then Haman said to King Ahasuerus, "There is a certain people scattered and dispersed among the people in all the provinces of your kingdom; their laws are different from all other people's, and they do not keep the king's laws. Therefore it is not fitting for the king to let them remain. If it pleases the king, let a decree be written that they be destroyed, and I will pay ten thousand talents of silver into the hands of those who do the work, to bring it into the king's treasuries."

A Root of Bitterness

In his book *Feelings: Our Vital Signs*, Dr. William Gaylin points out that "resentment often arises when we believe we aren't getting what is due us from another person. We feel unfairly cheated or betrayed. And brooding leads to all kinds of trouble."

Gaylin's description fits Haman perfectly. Because Mordecai refused to bow to him, Haman's resentment grew into bitterness. He became embittered not only with Mordecai but toward all those of Jewish descent. His bitterness festered until he was willing to pay 10,000 talents (about $20 million) of silver to extract his revenge.

Bitterness, however, costs much more

than money. It robs us of our health. Medical doctors link harboring resentments to such physical maladies as ulcers and high blood pressure.

But more than that, in the life of a Christian, bitterness destroys our intimacy with the Lord. The Bible teaches that bitterness is a sin (Eph. 4:31, Heb. 12:15). Unconfessed sin blocks our access to the Father and becomes a hindrance to our prayers (Isa. 1:11-16).

If you have allowed a spirit of bitterness to grow in your heart, confess it at once. Share your struggle with someone you trust. Do something kind for the one toward whom you've harbord bitter feelings. Whatever you do, don't allow a grudge to become a stumbling block in your walk with the Lord. Rip out every root of bitterness in your life and rediscover the joy of the Lord.

When the root is bitterness, imagine what the fruit might be.

Reflections/Prayer Requests

_____

_____

_____

DAY 15

Esther 4:1

When Mordecai learned all that had happened, he tore his clothes and put on sackcloth and ashes, and went out into the midst of the city. He cried out with a loud and bitter cry.

Good Grief

In the cartoon strip *Peanuts*, Charlie Brown often exclaims, "Good grief!" While he may not mean it in the literal sense, he is nevertheless right. Grief can be good. Studies show that those who express their anguish recover more quickly and are healthier as a result.

When Mordecai learned of the terrible fate being planned for his people, he grieved. Furthermore, he showed that grief in the traditional Jewish way—by donning sackcloth and ashes, lamenting loudly. Mordecai was not ashamed to show his sorrow. But neither did he let it sidetrack him. Following his expressions of grief, he took action.

Some Christians equate grief with a lack of faith. To them the unspoken rule is, "If you mourn, then you are implying that God is not good. Instead of grieving," they say, "just rejoice." But grief is a part of life, even for the most faithful.

The Bible certainly establishes parameters for our grief. The apostle Paul says, "But I do not want you to be ignorant, brethren, concerning those who have fallen asleep, lest you sorrow as others who have no hope" (1 Thess. 4:13). This verse does not exclude grief but instructs us to hope in the midst of it. Jesus Himself grieved at the tomb of His friend Lazarus (John 11:35) and even shed tears over the city of Jerusalem (Matt. 23:37). Certainly Jesus was not lacking in faith.

If you are grieving today, don't be ashamed of it. You are not an inferior or faithless Christian because you feel sorrow. Allow yourself the right to grief, but don't let grieve, rule your life. Grieve, grieve some more, and then get up and get on with your life. Until the day comes when all tears will be wiped away, there's nothing wrong with "good" grief.

We rejoice in spite of our grief, not in place of it.

Reflections/Prayer Requests

_____

_____

_____

_____

DAY 16

Esther 4:14

*"For if you remain completely silent
at this time, relief and deliverance will arise
for the Jews from another place, but you and
your father's house will perish. Yet who knows
whether you have come to the kingdom
for such a time as this?"*

For Such a Time As This

On October 3, 1991, Frederick Chiluba assumed power in Zambia's first democratic election, achieving a landslide victory. His first act as newly elected president was to call for a Celebration of Praise and to establish a Covenant with God before his people. He declared himself and his country subject to God's rule and asked for God's blessing. In 1996 he was reelected to the presidency of his African nation. God had His man at the right place at the right time.

History is filled with examples of God's perfect timing, but none is as dramatic as the story of Esther. Before anyone even knew about the need, God was preparing this young woman to be in the right place at the right time. Only a person with Esther's character, occupying a position as close to the throne as she did, could have accomplished the salvation of the Jewish people. God made sure it happened.

God is never caught unaware. When things develop at what may appear to us is a breakneck speed, God is always one step ahead. At the right time He maneuvers circumstances, removes obstacles and raises the right people to accomplish His will.

Sometimes the future can appear very uncertain. You may look at your situation and wonder how it's all going to work out. Don't allow yourself to be intimidated by the unknown. You have this assurance: at the right time and in the right place, God will provide for your need. If this is a troubling time for you, trust God. Even now He is preparing someone to help you for such a time as this.

If God was faithful to you yesterday, you have every reason to trust Him for tomorrow.

Reflections/Prayer Requests

_____

_____

_____

_____

_____

_____

DAY 17

Esther 4:16

*"Go, gather all the Jews
who are present in Shushan,
and fast for me; neither eat nor
drink for three days, night or day.
My maids and I will fast likewise.
And so I will go to the king, which is
against the law; and if I perish, I perish!"*

Give It All

General Charles Gordon served the British military conscientiously for many years in China. When the English government sought to reward him for his service, he declined all monetary remuneration but accepted a gold medal on which were inscribed his name and a record of his 31 engagements. At his death, the medal was missing. Later it was learned that during a famine in Manchester, he donated it to be melted and used to buy bread for the poor. In his diary that day he wrote these words: "The last and only thing that I had in this world that I valued, I have given over to the Lord Jesus Christ."

Esther, too, knew what it meant to give everything over to God—even her life. If being faithful to His calling meant she had to perish, she was willing. There was nothing that she would withhold from God's service. Life itself was less precious than the need to obey His will.

Others have followed in these same footsteps. Some had their lives spared, but others were killed. The writer of Hebrews says, "They were stoned, they were sawn in two, were tempted, were slain with the sword. They wandered about in sheepskins and goatskins, being destitute, afflicted, tormented; of whom the world was not worthy" (Heb. 11:37-38).

Giving your all to Jesus doesn't make you a martyr; it makes you a faithful disciple. Are you willing to give yourself and everything you possess to Jesus? Can you say with the hymn writer, "All to Jesus I surrender, All to Him I freely give"? If you can trust Him with your eternal soul, can you not trust Him with everything else you have, even your life?

We can't give our all to Jesus and keep some for ourselves.

Reflections/Prayer Requests

_____

_____

_____

_____

_____

DAY 18

Esther 5:2

So it was, when the king saw
Queen Esther standing in the court,
that she found favor in his sight, and the king
held out to Esther the golden scepter that was
in his hand. Then Esther went near and
touched the top of the scepter.

Finding Mercy

In the famous Rosenberg trial of the 1950s, Julius and Ethel Rosenberg were found guilty of treason and executed. In the closing arguments of that trial, the lawyer for the defendants pleaded, "Your Honor, what my clients ask for is justice." Judge Kaufman, the presiding judge for the case, replied, "The court has given what you ask for—justice! What you really want is mercy. But that is something this court has no right to give."

As Esther came before King Ahasuerus, she also hoped for more than justice. According to Persian law, to come into the presence of the king unbidden was a crime punishable by death. That was justice. What Esther sought, however, was mercy and fortunately the king had the right to grant it. Bestowing upon her the protection of his golden scepter, Ahasuerus granted her the privilege of standing in his presence without fear of execution.

The Christian has received this same kind of mercy from God. On our own, we deserve eternal death for our sins. Romans 6:23 says, "For the wages of sin is death." That would be nothing more than justice. Through Jesus Christ, however, God has extended mercy to us.. We can now stand before His very throne without fear of condemnation (Rom. 8:1)

As mercy has been given to us, let us give to others. Is there someone in your life who needs your mercy? Are you willing to give up your right to justice in order to show them mercy? Don't forget what the Scripture says: "Blessed are the merciful, for they shall obtain mercy" (Matt. 5:7).

Justice is for those who deserve it, mercy is for those who don't.

Reflections/Prayer Requests

_____

_____

_____

_____

_____

_____

DAY 19

Esther 5:3

*And the king said to her,
"What do you wish, Queen Esther?
What is your request?
It shall be given to you—
up to half my kingdom!"*

Ask and You Shall Receive

Among those who served in the court of Alexander the Great was a famous philosopher who had outstanding ability but little money. He asked Alexander for financial help and was told he could draw whatever cash he needed from the imperial treasury. Immediately he submitted to the treasurer a request for an amount equal to $50,000 today. The keeper of the funds was startled and said he couldn't give him that much money without a direct order. Going to Alexander, the treasurer argued that a small fraction of the money requested would be more appropriate. But the king replied, "Pay the money at once. This philosopher has done me a singular honor. By the large size of his request he shows that he has understood both my wealth and generosity."

King Ahasuerus showed an equally generous attitude toward Esther. He possessed enormous wealth and was willing to share it with her, even up to half of his enormous kingdom if she so desired.

Our Heavenly Father reflects this same bountifulness toward us. The apostle Paul wrote, "He who did not spare His own Son, but delivered Him up for us all, how shall He not with Him also freely give us all things?" (Romans 8:32). No request is too big for God.

Perhaps you feel your need is too great to ask for God's help. Maybe you even think you have already tapped God's generosity to the extreme. Could He possibly forgive you again for that same sin? Will He really provide for that astronomical need? The answer is yes! If your request is consistent with God's will, you need never worry about asking for too much. God delights in hearing from you.

Big gifts are the sign of a big God.

Reflections/Prayer Requests

_____

_____

_____

_____

_____

_____

DAY 20

Esther 5:11

Then Haman told them of his great riches, the multitude of his children, all the ways in which the king had promoted him, and how he had advanced him above the officials and servants of the king.

To Whom Credit Is Due

A proud woodpecker was tapping away at a dead tree when the sky unexpectedly turned black and the thunder began to roll. Undaunted, the woodpecker went right on working. Suddenly a bolt of lightning struck the old tree, splintering it into hundreds of pieces. Startled but unhurt, the haughty bird flew off, screeching to his feathered friends, "Hey, everyone, look what I did to that tree!"

Haman was a lot like that woodpecker. He was a man of many honors and much wealth. King Ahasuerus had promoted him to be chief among the princes of the Persian Empire (Esther 3:1). Sadly, along with the increase in his good fortune came an increase in his arrogance. Instead of giving credit to God, he called all his friends and family together and exclaimed, "Look what I've done!"

Too often we forget who really deserves the credit for our successes. Admittedly circumstances might give the appearances that we are responsible. Certainly we must use our intelligence and apply ourselves diligently. But even the assets of intellect and strength are from God. In addition, success is usually the result of factors beyond human control. Sometimes it's simply because God put us at the right place at the right time. If we view our success from this perspective, we begin to get some idea of how dependent we are on a power beyond ourselves—a power of God.

Success is enjoyable, but you'll enjoy it much more when you give God the credit. All that you have and all that you are is the direct result of His blessing. Don't forget to thank Him.

To sweeten success, try a little praise.

Reflections/Prayer Requests

_____

_____

_____

_____

_____

_____

DAY 21

Esther 5:14

*Then his wife Zeresh and all his
friends said to him, "Let a gallows be made,
fifty cubits high, and in the morning suggest
to the king that Mordecai be hanged on it;
then go merrily with the king to the banquet."
And the thing pleased Haman;
so he had the gallows made.*

How to Judge Advice

America's first "official" advice giver
was a woman whose pen name was
Dorothy Dix. Her first column appeared
July 11, 1896, in the *New Orleans Picayune*.
The column ran for 55 years. By the time of
her death in 1951, her column was carried
by nearly 300 papers. She was popularly
known as the "Mother Confessor to
Millions."

Miss Dix has been followed by a hoard of
others. We have Miss Manners, Dr. Joyce
Brothers, Dear Abby, her twin sister, Ann
Landers, and many more. In fact, most people relish the opportunity to give advice
either officially or unofficially. The chal-
lenge on our part is to know whether the
advice is good or bad.

Like you and me, Haman also had his
advice givers. His wife, Zeresh, and his
friends in the city of Shushan were more

than happy to play to Haman's pride and prejudices. But the advice they gave ultimately led to his destruction.

As Christians, our best advisor is the Word of God. God never sugarcoats His commandments to spare our feelings. We can always trust Him to tell us what is right, even if we don't want to hear it.

Wisdom dictates that we turn to others for counsel. The Bible says, "Listen to counsel and receive instruction, that you may be wise in your latter days" (Prov. 19:20). It also warns, "There are many plans in a man's heart, nevertheless the LORD's counsel—that will stand." There are many places and many people from whom you can get advice, but make sure the advice you're being given is consistent with God's counsel.

Free advice is sometimes the most costly kind.

Reflections/Prayer Requests

_____

_____

_____

_____

_____

DAY 22

Esther 6:2-3

And it was found written that Mordecai had told of Bigthana and Teresh, two of the king's eunuchs, the doorkeepers who had sought to lay hands on King Ahasuerus. Then the king said, "What honor or dignity has been bestowed on Mordecai for this?" And the king's servants who attended him said, "Nothing has been done for him."

Do Your Best

Several years ago, a crew of men was working on the road bed of a railroad when they were interrupted by a slow-moving train. The train stopped and a window in the last car—which was custom-made and air-conditioned—was raised. A friendly voice called out, "Dave, is that you?" Dave Anderson, the crew chief, called back, "Sure is, Jim. It's good to see you." With that pleasant exchange, Dave was invited to join Jim Murphy, the president of the railroad, for a visit.

After the train pulled out, Dave's crew surrounded him and expressed astonishment that he knew Mr. Murphy as a personal friend. Dave then explained that many years earlier he and Jim had started to work for the railroad on the same day. One man half jokingly asked Dave why he was still working out in the hot sun and Jim Murphy was now president. Wistfully Dave explained, "Twenty-three years ago I went to work for $1.75 an hour and Jim Murphy went to work for the railroad."

In the same way, when Mordecai became a court official, he went to work for the king, not just to draw a salary. His goal was not financial gain but to do the best job he possibly could. It was only natural, then, that when he discovered a plot on the king's life, he immediately reported it. He was loyal to the king and was only doing his job well.

Is your commitment to the paycheck or to the job? Are you fulfilling your duties to the best of your ability, or are you simply concerned about what you receive in return? Take your cue from Mordecai. Ask God to show you how you can honor Him through your employment.

✺

When you take care of your job, God will take care of the paycheck.

Reflections/Prayer Requests

_____

_____

_____

_____

DAY 23

Esther 6:6

So Haman came in,
and the king asked him,
"What shall be done for the man whom
the king delights to honor?" Now Haman
thought in his heart, "Whom would the
king delight to honor more than me?"

Look Before You Leap

Divers in Acapulco, Mexico, daily leap from the 87.5-foot-high La Quebrada cliff to the amazement of hundreds of gazing bystanders. In an extraordinary display of bravery, these daredevils risk death as they plunge into a rocky cove below only 12-feet deep. Their secret to success is that they carefully time their leap to coincide with incoming waves. When the waves are at their peak, they provide sufficient water to cushion the dive.

Haman could have profited from such an example before leaping to a conclusion that led to his humiliation. Eagerness to advance his own cause drove him to assume that it was he whom the king wanted to honor. Instead of receiving the privileges he proposed, however, he found himself honoring the man he hated the most, Mordecai.

The world is a dangerous place, especially for those prone to leap before they look. Scams abound even in religious circles. Too often miracle manipulaters, financial swindlers and false prophets have operated under the banner of Christianity. Cultists prey on those who are rash or careless. No wonder Jesus warned his disciples, "Behold, I send you out as sheep in the midst of wolves. Therefore be wise as serpents and harmless as doves" (Matt. 10:16).

In every area of your life—physical, spiritual, financial, emotional—look carefully before you take a plunge. Compare the claims made by people or groups with what the Bible says. Never assume because they carry the name "Church" or "Christian" that they faithfully adhere to the teachings of God's Word. Look before your leap. Be gentle, but by all means be wise!

The most dangerous leap is the leap to conclusions.

Reflections/Prayer Requests

DAY 24

Esther 7:5-6

*Then King Ahasuerus
answered and said to Queen Esther,
"Who is he, and where is he,
who would dare presume in his heart
to do such a thing?" And Esther said,
"The adversary and enemy is this wicked
Haman!" So Haman was terrified
before the king and queen.*

The Moment of Truth

One of the early television courtroom dramas was "Perry Mason." Each week Mr. Mason faced a baffling mystery that required solving before the end of the hour. Often the conclusion came as the guilty party sat in the witness stand. Buffeted by the astute lawyer's penetrating questions, the criminal's carefully constructed facade would crumble and his guilt would be exposed.

A similar drama took place in the palace of King Ahasuerus. Just when it seemed that Haman's wickedness would prevail, the tables were turned and his evil plot was revealed. When Esther pointed to him as the one who dreamed up the diabolical plan to destroy the Jewish people, Haman plunged from the height of arrogant pride to the depth of abject terror.

But such moments of stark truth are not limited to history or television. The Bible reveals that we all have a future appointment with God where He will reveal to us everything we have said, thought or done. Jesus said, "For there is nothing covered that will not be revealed, nor hidden that will not be known. Therefore whatever you have spoken in the dark will be heard in the light, and what you have spoken in the ear in inner rooms will be proclaimed on the housetops" (Luke 12:2-3).

Now is the time to prepare for that future appointment. Be careful about idle words you might speak or thoughtless deeds you might commit. Live in such a way that when the secrets of your life are revealed, they are either harmless or covered by the blood of Christ.

What's done in secret is never a secret to God.

Reflections/Prayer Requests

_____

_____

_____

_____

_____

DAY 25

Esther 7:8-10

*When the king returned
from the palace garden to the place of the
banquet of wine, Haman had fallen across
the couch where Esther was. Then the
king said, "Will he also assault the queen
while I am in the house?" As the word left
the king's mouth, they covered Haman's face.
Now Harbonah, one of the eunuchs, said
to the king, "Look! The gallows, fifty cubits
high, which Haman made for Mordecai,
who spoke good on the king's behalf,
is standing at the house of Haman."
Then the king said, "Hang him on it!"
So they hanged Haman on the gallows
that he had prepared for Mordecai.
Then the king's wrath subsided.*

The Slippery Slope

The fastest speed for a cross-country skier was set by Aleksey Prokurorov of Russia on March 19, 1994. Mr. Prokurorov maintained an average speed of 16.24 miles per hour for 50 kilometers. On the other hand, the speed record for downhill skiing belongs to Philippe Goitschel of France, who, on April 21, 1993, whizzed down the hill at 145.161 miles per hour. The drastic difference, of course, is caused by the slope.

Sin is also a slippery slope. In Psalm 73,

the psalmist says about the wicked, "Then I understood their end. Surely You set them in slippery places; You cast them down to destruction" (vv. 17-18).

When Haman plotted to destroy the Jews, he placed his feet on a slippery slope. Then, like a downhill skier out of control, he careened first through exposure, then condemnation and finally death.

Sin still operates that way today. Most people begin with small transgressions. Perhaps they shoplift a candy bar or rent an X-rated video. These sins seem rather small compared to bank robbery or rape. Yet they set the person's feet on the edge of a very slippery slope.

If Satan whispers in your ear, "Go ahead. It's only a little sin," tell him you know better. If you refuse to take lightly the minor transgressions, you'll be sure to avoid the major ones.

The best way to avoid going downhill is to stay off the slope.

Reflections/Prayer Requests

_____

_____

_____

DAY 26

Esther 8:1-2

*On that day King Ahasuerus gave
Queen Esther the house of Haman, the enemy
of the Jews. And Mordecai came before the king,
for Esther had told how he was related to her.
So the king took off his signet ring,
which he had taken from Haman, and gave it
to Mordecai; and Esther appointed Mordecai
over the house of Haman.*

From Rags to Riches

During the 1995 Christmas holidays, a passing motorist spotted a limousine stranded with a flat tire on a busy stretch of New Jersey highway. The man graciously stopped and offered to help the chauffeur change the tire. Just as the task was finished, the darkened window rolled down and the man inside asked what he and his wife could do to repay the favor. "Just send my wife a big bouquet of flowers," said the guy and handed him his card. Two weeks later a gargantuan bouquet of orchids arrived with a card reading, "We paid off your home mortgage. Marla and Donald Trump." Informers say the Trumps forked over more than $100,000 for the gesture.

Mordecai experienced a similar windfall. With the death of his enemy, Haman, he came into the possession of all Haman's wealth, one of Persia's highest officials. From the position of a minor bureaucrat, Mordecai suddenly became second only to the king.

Every Christian is graced with this same fortune. As unbelievers, we were spiritually impoverished. We owed a debt to God we could never repay. But when we trusted Jesus as Savior, we received the promise of His provision for our entire lifetime (Phil. 4:19). Even better, we were made spiritual billionaires when we became joint-heirs with Christ (Rom. 8:17).

Perhaps you are experiencing lean times. In spite of your efforts to be a good steward, too much month is left at the end of the paycheck. Don't despair. Trust God to meet your needs. These times of testing will someday give way to an abundance that is beyond your comprehension. You have God's word on it!

He is a poor man who can only measure his wealth in dollars.

Reflections/Prayer Requests

DAY 27

Esther 8:9-10

*So the king's scribes
were called at that time, in the
third month, which is the month of Sivan,
on the twenty-third day; and it was written,
according to all that Mordecai commanded. . . .
And he wrote in the name of King Ahasuerus,
sealed it with the king's signet ring, and sent
letters by couriers on horseback, riding on
royal horses bred from swift steeds.*

No Hurry

There is an old fable that tells of three apprentice devils who came to earth to finish their apprenticeship. They were talking to Satan, the chief of the devils, about their plans to tempt and ruin men. The first said, "I will tell them there is no God." Satan said, "That will not delude many, for they know there is a God." The second said, "I will tell men there is no hell." Satan answered, "You will deceive no one that way; men know even now that there is a hell for sin." The third said, "I will tell men there is no hurry." "You will ruin them by the thousand," said Satan. The most dangerous of all delusions is that there is plenty of time.

Mordecai suffered no such delusion. He knew he had to hurry if he were to effectively counteract Haman's deadly decree. With no waste of time, he called the scribes to record his words in the name of the king and then sent off messengers on swift horses to cover the 127 provinces of the vast empire. Urgency was of the utmost importance if he were to save the lives of his people.

As Christians, we have an equally urgent message. It is a message that explains how people perishing in their sins can be forgiven and receive eternal life. It is a proclamation of grace and mercy though the Lord Jesus Christ. Without it, multitudes will go into a Christless eternity.

Don't let Satan delude you. We don't have plenty of time. In fact, the time is short and the message is imperative. Ask God to show you how you can be used to spread the Good News before it's too late.

Don't snooze with the news.

Reflections/Prayer Requests

DAY 28

Esther 8:17

*And in every province and city,
wherever the king's
command and decree came,
the Jews had joy and gladness,
a feast and a holiday. Then many of
the people of the land became Jews,
because fear of the Jews
fell upon them.*

Good News

Have you noticed how much bad news you are hearing lately? Terrorism, corruption and murder fill the headlines. Such terms as "AIDS," the "Ebola virus" and "ethnic cleansing" have become household words. Many people long just to hear a little good news.

The Jews of Esther's time felt the same way. They were inundated with bad news. To their dismay, they learned that the wicked Haman had influenced the king to order their destruction. For months they lived with the threat of death hanging over their heads. Apprehensively, they watched as their enemies gathered around them like jackals waiting for a kill.

Then came the good news. Haman's plot had been foiled. Instead of being helpless victims, they were given the right to defend themselves. What was to have been their day of destruction became a day of victory instead. Weeping and mourning were thankfully replaced with rejoicing and celebrating.

To a world weary of bad news, Christians also have the privilege of sharing some wonderfully good news. The Good News of Christ proclaims that there is victory over the evil one, who would destroy us. No longer do we have to live without hope and in fear of death; we can rejoice and celebrate instead.

Since we live in a sinful world, there still will be plenty of bad news to talk about. But ask God to send someone across your path today who is tired of hearing bad news. Then share with him the good news that can be found only when you place your faith in Jesus Christ.

Let others report the bad news; we'll share the good news.

Reflections/Prayer Requests

DAY 29

Esther 9:20-22

*And Mordecai wrote these things
and sent letters to all the Jews . . .
to establish among them that they should
celebrate yearly the fourteenth and fifteenth
days of the month of Adar, . . . as the month
which was turned from sorrow to joy for them,
and from mourning to a holiday.*

Joy Comes in the Morning

Life is filled with horror and tragedies. On September 1, 1939, Germany invaded Poland and began a systematic annihilation of the Jewish people. During the years of the Holocaust, approximately 65 to 70 percent of all European Jews perished. In 1975 a group of rebels called the Khmer Rouge took control in Cambodia. Tens of thousands died under their harsh treatment. In 1994 the Rwandan president died in a plane crash under mysterious circumstances. Within a month an estimated 200,000 people in Rwanda died from violence unleashed by racial hatred.

The Jewish people in Esther's time were faced with tragedy as well. As Haman's plan for ethnic cleansing was proclaimed throughout the empire, grief enveloped the land. God's people responded with tears and cries of sorrow. What they didn't know was that even as they lamented, God was in the process of engineering their deliverance. In the midst of their darkest night, God was preparing a joyous morning.

Christians are not immune from such tragedies. Brian O'Connell, director of the Religious Liberty Commission of the World Evangelical Fellowship, claims, "More Christians have been martyred in the twentieth century than in the previous nineteen combined." This is horrifying, but our comfort comes from knowing there will be a joyous morning.

If you are experiencing a great sorrow, rest assured that God is preparing a time of joyous celebration. The psalmist says, "Weeping may endure for a night, but joy comes in the morning" (Ps. 30:5). When the morning of Christ's return breaks, sadness will be swallowed up by an everlasting joy.

God's dawn always follows grief's darkness.

Reflections/Prayer Requests

_____

_____

_____

_____

_____

DAY 30

Esther 9:26-28

*So they called these days Purim,
after the name Pur. Therefore, because of all
the words of this letter, what they had seen
concerning this matter, and what had happened to them, the Jews established and
imposed it upon themselves and their descendants and all who would join them, that without fail they should celebrate these two days
every year, according to the written instructions
and according to the prescribed time, . . .
that the memory of them should not perish
among their descendants.*

Just a Reminder

Do you know what these words have in common: Tishri, Kislev, Nisan, Sivan and Ab? They are months in the Jewish calen-dar. For the devout Jew, the calendar is more than a way of marking time—it pro-vides a convenient method of recalling God's dealings in their life. Nisan marks Passover, the time of Israel's deliverance from Egyptian bondage. Sivan brings the Feast of Pentecost, the celebration of a bountiful harvest from God. Tishri reminds the people of their wilderness wanderings through the Feast of the Tabernacles. Each holiday becomes a holy day, a time of recalling, repenting and renewing old com-mitments to follow the God of Israel.

During the days of Esther, yet another special time of remembrance was added to the Jewish calendar. Each year, on the 14th and 15th day of the month of Adar, the people celebrate God's victory over evil, Haman's attempt to exterminate the Jews. It is called the Feast of Purim.

As Christians we have our own special times of remembrance. At Christmas we remember Christ's birth, and on Easter we remember His death and resurrection. More frequently, we celebrate together the memory of His sacrifice at Calvary. We call it the Lord's Supper or Communion.

It's good to take advantage of every opportunity you have to remember what God has done for you. Enjoy Christmas, Easter, Sunday and every Lord's Supper celebration. Be sensitive to the spiritual truths behind these occasions. None of us have such good memories that we don't need reminders.

When God does it, we do more than remember it—we celebrate it.

Reflections/Prayer Requests

_____

_____

_____

DAY 31

Esther 10:3

*For Mordecai the Jew
was second to King Ahasuerus,
and was great among the Jews and well
received by the multitude of his brethren,
seeking the good of his people and speaking
peace to all his kindred.*

Dedicated to Service

John Brodie, former quarterback for the San Francisco 49ers, was once asked why a million-dollar player such as he should have to hold the ball for field goals and extra-points attempts. "Well," said Brodie, "if I didn't, it would fall over." There is something appealing about this kind of humility in service. We see in it a reflection of true greatness.

Mordecai had this kind of appeal as well. He became great among his people, but not because he held a position second only to the king. He was well received by the multitude, but not because he was rich or related to the queen. Mordecai's true greatness came because he had a heart dedicated to service. The wicked Haman had used his office to promote himself; Mordecai used his position to bring good to his people.

Throughout history, greatness has been

associated with unselfish service. When H. M. Stanley went to Africa in 1871 to find David Livingstone, he found Livingstone engaged in untiring service for those whom he had no reason to love except for Christ's sake. Stanley wrote in his journal, "When I saw that unwearied patience, that unflagging zeal and those enlightened sons of Africa, I became a Christian at his side, though he never spoke to me one word."

While the world may never classify you as a John Brodie the quarterback, a Mordecai the Jew or a David Livingstone the missionary, you can still be great with God. Find the place He would have you serve, and serve Him until you die.

It's not important how many people you lead, but how many you serve.

Reflections/Prayer Requests

a Good Book! LA 10-11-97

_____

_____

_____

_____

_____

_____